On the Level
Foundations for Violence-Free Living

created by the Wilder Men's Domestic Abuse Program
written by David J. Mathews, MS, LICSW

FIELDSTONE
ALLIANCE

SAINT PAUL
MINNESOTA

We thank the Bigelow Foundation of St. Paul, Minnesota,
for their contribution toward the development of this curriculum.

Fieldstone Alliance
60 Plato Boulevard East, Suite 150
Saint Paul, MN 55107

800-274-6024
www.FieldstoneAlliance.org

For more information about the Amherst H. Wilder Foundation's Community Assistance Program, please call 651-221-0048 or visit www.wilder.org.

Curriculum developed by the staff of Wilder Community
    Assistance Program
Written by David J. Mathews
Edited by Vincent Hyman
Designed by Rebecca Andrews
Cover illustration by Greg Preslicka

Manufactured in the United States of America
Fourth printing, May 2007

ISBN-13: 978-0-940069-06-0
ISBN-10: 0-940069-06-7

 Printed on recycled paper

Introduction

Men's violence has been with us for a long time. We've hurt, injured, even killed our brothers, wives, partners, and others who have crossed us in moments of anger and rage. The goal before us is not to cast blame, but rather to put a stop to the violence. We need to take responsibility for ourselves, our actions, and our words. There are no winners in violence, only pain, suffering, and loss.

I'm sure if you are reading this introduction there are many things going through your mind. What you are about to undertake might be one of the most difficult tasks you'll ever face in your life.

You will be asked to openly and honestly look at yourself, as you've never done before—not to find fault, but to find truth.

It will take a great deal of inner strength and courage. Much of what you've thought, done, felt, or believed about yourself and others will be questioned. The ways in which you've lived your past and your beliefs about the future will be challenged.

While these questions and challenges might be asked and made by others, the answers must come from within. Only *you* can determine the lessons you will learn. You alone will make the choices. You alone will make the changes.

The mind is like a parachute—it only works when it's open.

Some men will refuse to pull the cord to open the parachute. They'll never take the opportunity to look around and see what might be seen—to change what could be changed.

Other men may only open their parachute for a brief moment, then quickly draw it closed. They'll fall short, never knowing what could have been.

Yet those men who are willing to keep the parachute open, to look at themselves no matter how difficult it gets, will see their lives change. They can end their abuse. They can live a life free of violence.

It won't be easy—but it will be worth it.

Michael F. McGrane
Director and Founder
Amherst H. Wilder Foundation's Men's Domestic Abuse Program

Contents

About This Workbook

Here are some commonly asked questions about this workbook and program. If you have further questions, talk to your group leader right away.

1. *What is the purpose of this workbook?*

   This workbook is yours to remind you of what you are learning and the progress you are making. It also helps the group leader to better understand your point of view. It is *not* a test. There are no right or wrong answers. What you write will probably be very different from what others write. You won't be graded on spelling or grammar or anything else. Keep your responses readable, but you may doodle and take notes wherever you wish. We hope that this workbook will help you see further progress and growth as you continue to address life issues after completing this program.

2. *Why are there so many pages in this workbook?*

   Everything you need is in this workbook. We designed it so that you don't have to do any outside reading (unless assigned by your group leader). Also, there are more activities here than you probably will use, so your group leader can pick the exercises that will be most helpful to the group. It will take some work on your part to fill in the workbook, but don't expect to use all the pages.

3. *Who will see my workbook?*

   This workbook is your private account. What you write here is for YOU. The only other person to see it will be your group leader (or leaders). You will be able to keep the workbook after completing the program.

4. *When should I ask questions?*

   Ask your group leader if you are confused or uncertain about anything. If you do not understand a question or an assignment, ASK! If you have difficulty reading or writing, tell the group leader. The group leader will make arrangements so you can complete the program.

5. *When should I bring this workbook?*

   Bring this workbook to every session. At each session, the group leader may assign some workbook pages. If you miss a session, find out what happened. Be sure to ask what assignments you must prepare for the following session as well as the session you missed.

6. *What about my rights, responsibilities, and confidentiality?*

   You and the other men in the group will develop some guidelines for respectful behavior and expectations of each other. If you have further questions about the forms you signed when you met with your counselor, talk to your group leader.

Goals

In this activity, you will:

1. Understand the purpose and nature of this program.

2. Begin to feel less isolated as a man who has been abusive.

3. Become comfortable in the group setting.

4. Develop, as a group, expectations for behavior within the group.

5. Develop, as a group, goals for what members want to learn and discuss.

6. Begin to talk with other men who have been abusive.

Required Worksheet

Getting to Know Other Group Members (Worksheet 1)

Notes

1. His first name:_____
    - Who the abuse was against: _____
    - One thing he wants to get out of the group meetings: _____
      _____
    - A personal strength: _____

2. His first name:_____
    - Who the abuse was against: _____
    - One thing he wants to get out of the group meetings: _____
      _____
    - A personal strength: _____
      _____

3. His first name:_____
    - Who the abuse was against: _____
    - One thing he wants to get out of the group meetings: _____
      _____
    - A personal strength: _____
      _____

Goals

In this activity, you will:

1. Learn and understand the program's philosophical basis.

2. Discuss whether you agree with the eight program principles.

3. Talk more with other men in the group.

4. Begin to develop your own philosophy of violence and abuse.

Required Worksheets

Eight Program Principles (Worksheet 2)

My Philosophy of Abuse and Violence (Worksheet 3)

Notes

1. Violence has rewards and consequences.

   What are some rewards?

   What are some consequences?

2. Violence can be passed on from generation to generation.

   How?

3. Violence is reinforced by our society.

   In what ways?

4. Violence can be unlearned. There are other ways to express feelings. There are alternatives to controlling people and situations.

   What are some alternatives?

5. I am responsible for my behavior.

   In what ways?

6. Provocation does not justify violence.

   When is violence justified?

7. 100 percent rule: I am 100 percent responsible for my side of a relationship.

   When are you *not* responsible for your behavior in the relationship?

8. The only person I can control is myself.

   Who else can I control? When?

Describe your philosophy of abuse and violence below.

1. Abuse means:

2. Violence means:

3. People are abusive because:

4. How does society view abuse and violence? How can you tell?

5. How do the media (newspapers, television, radio, commercials, magazines, advertisements) show violence and abuse?

6. Why do people continue to be abusive?

7. When, if at all, is it okay for you to be abusive or violent?

8. What are your rewards for abuse and violence in the above situations?

9. What are possible negative consequences in these situations?

10. In what specific situations is it okay for you to hurt someone? When does a person deserve to be abused?

11. How much is a person responsible for his or her own behavior?

12. If person A abuses person B, who is to blame for the abuse?

13. What, if any, are the reasons to blame the abused person or both
    people for the abuse?

14. How much can one person control another person?

Men's Rules about Men

Goals

In this activity, you will:

1. Identify some messages about how men should or should not act.

2. Understand how these messages influence your behaviors.

3. Identify the advantages and disadvantages of believing in and acting on these messages.

4. Identify your beliefs about who men are and how men should act.

5. Identify society's expectations and your personal beliefs about how women should or should not act.

6. Understand how these beliefs affect your behaviors toward women.

7. Increase your awareness of sexist attitudes and how they affect men's behaviors toward women.

8. List and increase alternative, positive messages about being a man.

Required Worksheets

Men's Rules about Men (Worksheet 4)
Men's Rules about Women (Worksheet 5)
Summary of Men's Rules (Worksheet 6)

Notes

1. List society's rules, traditions, and messages that define how a man should act, think, or be. Also list examples of how a man should *not* act, think, or be. How are men shown in the media (commercials, movies, cartoons)? Who are boys' heroes? Examples of such rules include: *Men should not cry. Men should not show their emotions. Men need to be in control.*

2. List the messages your family gave you about being a man. List the messages about how a man should act. Who were your heroes when growing up? How did these heroes get the job done?

3. List your rewards for maintaining and living by these rules.
    What do you gain from these rules?

4. List the consequences of following these rules.
    What do you lose or miss out on?

5. Do you find more rewards or negative consequences for the rules? If there
    are more rewards, why change your attitude? List some rewards you may
    receive if you challenge these rules.

6. List some negative consequences of breaking Men's Rules about Men.

7. What are some better rules and attitudes for men? How can you encourage these attitudes in yourself? Where will you get support for believing and acting on these new attitudes?

8. How can you encourage more positive attitudes about men among other men? Among boys, such as sons and nephews?

1. What are men's expectations and rules about how women should act and think? Examples of such rules include: *Women need to be protected. Women are the weaker sex.*

2. List your beliefs about women: How they should act, think, and be. How similar is this list to the list of men's expectations of women?

3. How can you encourage more positive attitudes among men toward women? What might you say to a male friend of yours who makes a sexist comment or who puts down a woman? Would your reactions change if the woman he was putting down was your mother? Your sister? Your daughter?

Compare all of your lists of attitudes toward women and men.

1. What are the similarities?

2. What are the differences?

3. Which expectations are realistic?

4. Which expectations are unrealistic?

5. How are your attitudes about women and men affected by society?

6. How do you view women? Negatively? Positively?

7. How do you demonstrate these attitudes? (For example, do you tell jokes that
    put women down? Do you believe women are bad and out to get men? Do you
    tell a male friend that you are offended by his remarks that put women
    down? Would you call 911 if you hear or see a man abusing a woman?)

8. How do you want your daughter to relate to men when she is an adult?

9. What are your attitudes toward your mother, wife, girlfriend, women coworkers, women you meet casually?

10. What are the differences in how you view these women? What are the similarities?

House of Abuse

Goals

In this activity, you will:

1. Extend the definition of abuse beyond the four categories of verbal, physical, emotional, and sexual.

2. Identify the purpose of abusive behaviors.

3. Increase your personal awareness of abusive behaviors.

4. Understand that changing abusive behavior is an ongoing process.

5. Understand that abuse is abuse no matter what form it takes.

Required Worksheet

House of Abuse (Worksheet 7)

Notes

1. List examples of the types of abuse in each room.

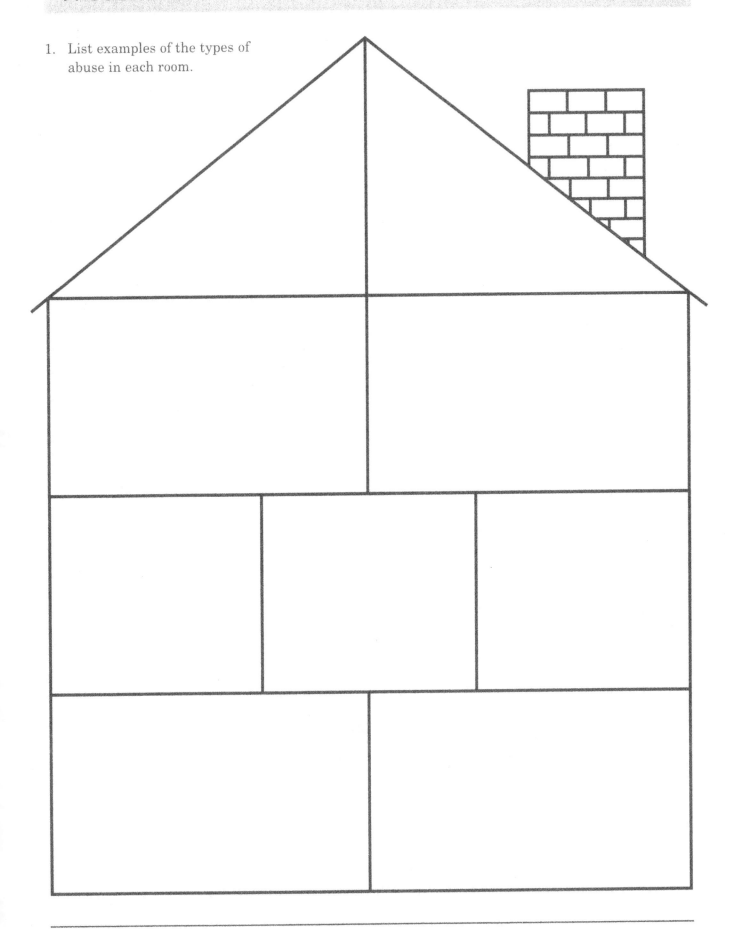

2. How are the rooms similar? How are they connected?

3. What would happen if you totally cleaned out three or four rooms but left the other rooms full?

4. How does abuse support power and control?

5. What is in the basement of your house? What are the feelings?

6. Are there other rooms you could add to the house?

7. What feelings do you have when you see this house full of abuse?

8. What have you learned from looking at abuse this way?

9. What do you need to do to clean your house and how can you take care of yourself in this process?

Goals

In this activity, you will:

1. Better understand how abuse happens again and again.

2. Learn the three stages of the abuse cycle and what these stages look like.

3. Understand at what points you need to make new decisions so no abuse occurs.

The Pattern of Abuse

Required Worksheet

Pattern of Abuse (Worksheet 8)

Notes

Draw your own pattern of abusive behavior. Show the escalation, blowout, after behaviors, and how the pattern begins again. Use stick figures, symbols, numbers, words, designs, or whatever makes sense to you.

Goals

In this activity, you will:

1. Identify what you think and feel and how your body reacts when you begin to get angry or upset.

2. Identify words, phrases, sentences, subject matter, situations, or times of the day when you feel confused, tense, angry, or upset.

3. Increase your willingness to accept what other people tell you about your behavior.

Required Worksheets

Escalation Signals (Worksheet 9)

Feelings Words (Worksheet 10)

Signals Monitoring Log (Worksheet 11)

Notes

Make a list of the signals (or cues) that you are getting upset.

1. *Physical Signals*. When you get angry, how does your body react?
   What is your body telling you? What are you doing?

2. *Thought Signals*. What suspicions, assumptions, thoughts, and self-talk
   get you upset?

3. *Emotional Signals.* What feelings do you have before and during the times when you are upset? What feelings do you have before and during the times when you are verbally, physically, or sexually abusive? Use the Feelings Words worksheet to help you identify your feelings.

4. *Red Flag Words and Sentences.* What words, phrases, and sentences get you upset?

5. *Red Flag Situations.* What are the "hot" situations, topics, places, and times of day?

Emotional signals are the feelings you have before, during, or after the times that you are abusive. There are names for these signals. "Angry" or "upset" are the easy ones. Try to identify the most exact name for the feeling you are having by looking at the list of feelings under the category for that feeling.

Happy	Sad		Angry	Scared	Confused
Excited	Devastated	Disheartened	Strangled	Fearful	Bewildered
Elated	Hopeless	Despised	Furious	Panicky	Trapped
Exuberant	Sorrowful	Disappointed	Seething	Afraid	Immobilized
Ecstatic	Depressed	Upset	Enraged	Shocked	Directionless
Terrific	Wounded	Inadequate	Hostile	Overwhelmed	Stagnant
Jubilant	Hurt	Dismal	Vengeful	Intimidated	Flustered
Enthusiastic	Drained	Unappreciated	Incensed	Desperate	Baffled
Loved	Defeated	Discouraged	Abused	Frantic	Constricted
Thrilled	Exhausted	Ashamed	Hateful	Terrified	Troubled
Uplifted	Helpless	Distressed	Humiliated	Vulnerable	Ambivalent
Marvelous	Crushed	Distant	Sabotaged	Horrified	Awkward
Justified	Worthless	Disillusioned	Betrayed	Petrified	Puzzled
Resolved	Uncared-for	Lonely	Repulsed	Appalled	Disorganized
Valued	Dejected	Neglected	Rebellious	Full of dread	Foggy
Gratified	Rejected	Resigned	Pissed off	Tormented	Perplexed
Encouraged	Humbled	Islanded	Outraged	Tense	Hesitant
Optimistic	Empty	Regretful	Fuming	Threatened	Torn
Joyful	Miserable	Alienated	Exploited	Uneasy	Misunderstood
Proud	Distraught	Isolated	Throttled	Defensive	Doubtful
Cheerful	Deserted	Drained	Mad	Insecure	Bothered
Relieved	Grievous	Slighted	Spiteful	Skeptical	Undecided
Assured	Burdened	Degraded	Patronized	Apprehensive	Uncomfortable
Determined	Demoralized	Deprived	Vindictive	Suspicious	Uncertain
Grateful	Condemned	Disturbed	Used	Alarmed	Surprised
Appreciated	Terrible	Abandoned	Repulsed	Shaken	Unsettled
Confident	Unwanted	Sorry	Ridiculed	Swamped	Unsure
Respected	Unloved	Lost	Resentful	Startled	Distracted
Admired	Mournful	Bad	Disgusted	Guarded	
Accepted	Pitiful	Disenchanted	Smothered	Stunned	
Amused	Discarded	Deflated	Frustrated	Awed	
Delighted	Disgraced	Apathetic	Stifled	Reluctant	
Alive			Offended	Anxious	
Fulfilled			Controlled	Impatient	
Tranquil			Peeved	Shy	
Content			Annoyed	Nervous	
Relaxed			Agitated	Unsure	
Glad			Irritated	Timid	
Good			Exasperated	Concerned	
Satisfied			Harassed	Perplexed	
Peaceful			Anguished	Doubtful	
Hopeful			Deceived		
Fortunate			Aggravated		
Pleased			Perturbed		
Flattered			Provoked		
			Dominated		
			Coerced		
			Cheated		
			Uptight		
			Dismayed		
			Tolerant		
			Displeased		

1. Who can you ask to observe your behavior and tell you what they see?

2. Name one or more feelings you want to monitor to help you learn about your escalation signals:

3. During the next two weeks, log your signals in the chart on the next page every time you experience the feeling you want to monitor. Write into the next box if you need more room. Make a new chart if you run out of space.

Date	What you are thinking	How your body is reacting	Your feelings	Your red flag words and phrases	Your red flag situations and subjects

Goals

In this activity, you will:

1. Increase the use of nonabusive options when dealing with feelings that have led to the desire to control your partner.

2. Develop a plan with several options to stop yourself from escalating to abuse.

3. Develop a respectful plan to communicate with your partner or ex-partner.

4. Understand the obstacles to leaving an argument and develop some techniques to overcome those obstacles.

Required Worksheets

Responsibility Plan (Worksheet 12)

Responsibility Plan Monitoring Worksheet (Worksheet 13)

Notes

1. Things to do to avoid becoming abusive

    a. *Previous actions.* (Things you have done in the past to help yourself deal with your feelings in a nonabusive way.)

    b. *Obstacles to leaving.* (What beliefs or self-talk keep you from taking a time-out?)

    c. *Alternative self-talk.* (What positive things have you said to yourself to get past the obstacles?)

2. The time-out plan

    *   What signals tell you that you need a time-out?

    *   What will you do or say to leave in a positive way?

    *   What will you say to yourself (positive self-talk) to help you leave?

    *   Where will you go, what will you do, and how long will you be gone?

        Option A:

        Option B:

        Option C:

- People you can contact who will help you cool down:

  Option A:

  Option B:

  Option C:

3. The reconnecting plan

    - What signals within yourself will tell you that you are ready to approach your partner in a respectful manner?

    - What can you do or say to reconnect in a way that is respectful of your partner and yourself?

_____ *I have explained this plan to my current partner.*

(date)

Each time you use your plan in the next three weeks, record the following. Write over the boxes if you need more space.

Date	What the situation was	What you were thinking before the situation	How you were feeling before the situation	What you were thinking during the situation	How you were feeling during the situation	What you were thinking after the situation	How you were feeling after the situation

Most Violent Behavior

Goals

In this activity, you will:

1. Better understand how your past abusive behaviors affect your relationships, other people, and yourself.

2. Talk specifically about your abusive behaviors, including what you did, how you felt, and what you were thinking.

3. Begin (or continue) the healing process in your life.

4. Deal directly with your feelings about your own behaviors.

5. Begin to take responsibility for your abusive behaviors.

6. Understand how to use what you've learned about your current and past behaviors to avoid being abusive in the future.

7. Reveal your attitudes about your behaviors to other members of the group—and to yourself.

8. Describe your most violent behavior from your point of view.

Required Worksheet

My Most Violent Behavior (Worksheet 14)

Notes

Describe the situation in which you were the most abusive with a spouse, significant other, or partner. Include what happened before the situation began. What specifically did you argue about? What sort of names or words were used? How long ago did this happen?

Identify your pattern of being abusive during this situation:

- Your signals and escalation:

- What you were thinking:

- What you were feeling:

- What abuse you committed:

- What injuries your partner received:

- What you were thinking as you were being abusive:

- What you were feeling as you were being abusive:

- What happened after you were abusive:

- What you were thinking after you were abusive:

- How you felt after you were abusive:

Follow-up questions

How do you feel when you think about what you did to her?

In what ways did your abusive behavior in this situation affect you:
- physically (for example, did your hand hurt, or did you have a hangover?)

- socially

- intellectually

- spiritually

- emotionally

- sexually

In what ways did your abusive behavior in this situation affect the relationship:

- physically

- socially

- intellectually

- spiritually

- emotionally

- sexually

In what ways did your abusive behavior in this situation affect others (family, children)?

What have you gained in the relationship by doing these abusive behaviors?

What have you lost?

What will you need to do to gain support for who you are as a person?

What specific behaviors will you need to change in this relationship because of the abusive actions you used with your partner?

What changes do you need to make (or have you already made) that might restore this relationship? Does your partner want to restore the relationship?

What are you not able to change?

When she brings up the subject of your abusive behavior, how will you feel? What self-talk will you need to use? How can you respond in a positive, nonviolent manner?

What have you learned about your behavior and yourself from this situation?

Control
Strategies

Goals

In this activity, you will:

1. Better understand what control is.

2. Identify the methods you have used to control others.

3. Better understand that the only person you can control is yourself.

4. Develop a control monitoring system to help you practice alternatives to controlling people.

5. Develop a self-control support network.

Required Worksheet

Control Strategies (Worksheet 15)
Control Monitoring System (Worksheet 16)

Notes

1. What does the word "control" mean to you?

2. Names of people you have tried to control:

    a.

    b.

    c.

    d.

3. What you have done to try to control others:

    a.

    b.

    c.

4. What people, things, or situations can't you control in your life?

5. What do you gain by trying to control these people or things?

6. What do you gain by "letting go" of trying to control others?

    a.

    b.

    c.

7. It hurts when you realize you can't control others. How can you address the feelings of loss for not being able to control people or situations?

8. What *can* you control in your life?

   a.

   b.

   c.

9. Who will support your efforts to focus on the things you can control in your life? Where can you go to get support for those efforts?

10. List some nonviolent alternatives you can use when you realize you are trying to control another person:

   a.

   b.

   c.

Date	Situation	People involved	Your feelings	What you wanted to control	What you did to get control	Alternative strategies for future situations

Goals

In this activity, you will:

1. Define male privilege.

2. Understand the role of male privilege in society and in relationships with partners.

3. Recognize the rewards and consequences of male privilege

4. Develop some alternatives to the use of male privilege.

Required Worksheet

Male Privilege (Worksheet 17)

Notes

1. What does power mean?

2. How is male privilege demonstrated in our society?

3. How do you get power?

Physically	Emotionally	Intellectually	Spiritually	Socially

4. How does your male privilege in society affect others?

5. What do you gain from maintaining your privilege as a male in society?

6. What sort of privileges do you have as a man in this society?

7. In what ways does a man have more power than a woman in a relationship?

8. What do you gain from maintaining your power as a male in your relationship?

9. What will you gain by sharing or letting go of this power?

10. What will you lose by sharing or letting go of this power?

11. How can you support yourself when grieving over this loss of power?

12. How and where can you become empowered?

Family of Origin

Goals

In this activity, you will:

1. Better understand how your family of origin affects your behavior, particularly abusive behavior.

2. Understand that even though your family of origin may have influenced your decision to be violent, you are still responsible for your violent actions.

3. Understand the messages you received as a child that modeled abusive ways of solving problems.

4. Better understand those experiences that affected your feelings, thoughts, and behaviors while growing up.

5. Become more aware of the attitudes you were exposed to as a child that carry over into adulthood, particularly attitudes about women.

Required Worksheets

Family Tree (Worksheet 18)
Family of Origin (Worksheet 19)

Notes

Draw a family tree showing who was in your family and how you were related. Include divorces, deaths, stepparents, stepbrothers, and stepsisters. Include as many relatives as you can remember, and reach as far back as you can remember. Also include any friends of the family who were especially close or influential.

1. Who did you grow up with?

2. What is your overall feeling about growing up in your family—happy, fearful, sad, angry? What experiences contributed to these feelings?

3. What do you remember about how your mother was treated by her partner (your father, stepfather, or mother's partner)?

4. Who had the most power in your family when you were growing up?
    How did you know this person had the most power?

5. Some of the rules around the house were:

6. Who usually punished you when you were growing up?

7. When you were disciplined as a child:

    a. What did your father do?

    b. When he did this, how did you feel?

    c. What did your mother do?

    d. When she did this, how did you feel?

8. How did your mother or father usually punish you? How did you feel
    when punished this way?

9. What is your overall feeling about your school experience?
   What experiences contributed to these feelings?

10. Growing up, when did you feel the most comfortable and safe?
    How old were you?

11. Who did you look up to most when you were growing up?
    Why did you look up to this person?

12. When growing up . . .

   a.   I thought girls were:

   b.   I thought boys could:

   c.   when it came to sex, I thought boys should:

   d.   when it came to sex, I thought girls should:

   e.   I thought boys' friends should always be:

   f.   I thought boys should always play with:

   g.   I thought men should always:

   h.   I thought women should always:

13. Who taught you what it meant to be a man?
    What did you like about this person?

14. Name one thing you swore you would *never* do when you grew up:

15. How has this thought affected your behavior?

16. Who showed you it was okay to be violent? Who showed you how to use abuse as a way to solve problems?

17. What negative, unhealthy attitudes or behaviors have you learned from others?

18. What can you do to change these unhealthy learned behaviors and attitudes?

Goals

In this activity, you will:

1. Understand that alcohol and other drug use does not cause domestic abuse but may play a part in it.

2. Make a list of personal signals that show you may start drinking or using other drugs.

3. Understand the personal consequences of your alcohol or other drug use.

4. Develop a plan to remain free of alcohol and other drugs as part of your goal of refraining from domestic abuse.

Required Worksheets

Alcohol and Other Drugs (Worksheet 20)

Staying Free of Alcohol and Other Drugs (Worksheet 21)

Notes

1. How often do you drink alcohol or use other drugs? What substances do you use?

2. List reasons why you use alcohol or other drugs:

3. What signals tell you that you may drink or use other drugs:

Situations	Time of day	People you are with	Your feelings	Your thoughts

4. How do you act when you drink or use other drugs?

5. What consequences result from your chemical use? What are your losses?

6. List and describe the situations in which you have been drinking or using other drugs and have become abusive:

7. Who has expressed concern about your use of alcohol or other drugs?

8. What do these concerns and consequences mean to you?

1. List your signals before using alcohol or other drugs:

2. List the messages you can give yourself about the possible consequences if you were to start using alcohol or other drugs:

3. List three alternatives to using alcohol or other drugs:

   a.

   b.

   c.

4. Name three people you can contact or talk with about alcohol and other
   drug use:

   a.

   b.

   c.

5. List other ways to stay sober or receive support for staying free of
   alcohol and other drugs:

Goals

In this activity, you will:

1. Increase your understanding of how abusive behavior affected your sexual relationship.

2. Increase your awareness of your attitudes about sexuality.

3. Better understand how attitudes about sexuality affect nonviolent problem solving.

4. Better understand your perspective on and values about sexuality.

Required Worksheet

Sex and Sexuality (Worksheet 22)

Notes

1. How have women been treated as sex objects in the media and by society? (Give examples.)

2. Words and phrases that are used to describe men and men's genitals:

3. Words and phrases that are used to describe women and women's genitals:

4. What are the differences between the two lists?

5. With regards to sex how were boys supposed to act on a date?

6. With regards to sex how were girls supposed to act on a date?

7. What conflicts have you had with partners about being sexual?

8. If you wanted to be sexual and your partner didn't, what would you do?

9. What would she do?

10. If she wanted to be sexual and you didn't, what would you do?

11. What would she do?

12. How have your abusive behaviors affected your sexual relationship with your partner?

13. What are the signals that your abusive behavior is affecting your sexual relationship?

14. Using the assertive approach, develop nonabusive ways to handle the following situations:

    a. You are watching TV, about ready to go to bed, and feel like being sexual with your partner. You ask her about it, and she begins to argue with you. She says, "You always want sex whenever you want it, and never consider me."

    b. It has been three months since you and your partner have been sexual together. You say, "Let's have some fun tonight." She says she can't forget about the last time you got violent with her, so she doesn't want to "have fun tonight."

Goals

In this activity, you will:

1. Better understand how your abusive behaviors have affected others.

2. Take increased responsibility for your abusive behaviors.

3. Gain insight into why you have been abusive.

Required Worksheet

Letters to the People I Have Abused (Worksheet 23)

Notes

There are two reasons to write letters to the people you have abused. One is to gain more insight into your behavior. The other is to begin to take more responsibility for your actions. You don't have to mail these letters.

List all the people you have directly or indirectly abused in any way or form:

- _____   - _____
- _____   - _____
- _____   - _____
- _____   - _____
- _____   - _____

Circle the names of those people you will write a letter to (at least two).

Here are some questions to think about when you write this letter:

- What abuse did you do?
- How do you feel about what you did?
- How did you feel when you were escalating in these situations?
- How are your partner and kids affected by your abusive actions? (How might she feel, what might she think you will do to her in the future, what did she have to stop or change in order for you to get your way, how did her life have to change?)
- What are you doing to take responsibility for your abusive actions?
- What do you want from these people now?

After you have written the letters, answer the following questions:

- If you send these letters, how might the other people be affected?

- How would you feel if you sent these letters?

Goals

In this activity, you will:

1. Better understand how to be accountable for your abusive behaviors.

2. Take responsibility for your abusive behaviors.

3. Develop a plan to be responsible and accountable for your abusive behaviors.

Personal Accountability Plan

Required Worksheet

Personal Accountability Plan (Worksheet 24)

Notes

1. What is accountability?

2. Accountability Diagram 1

   (Who are you accountable to at work, at home, in society, on the street?)

                                   YOU

3. Accountability Diagram 2

    (Who are you accountable to for your abusive behaviors?)

YOU

4. How does it feel to be accountable to people?

5. How can you benefit from being accountable for your abusive behaviors?

6. Personal Accountability Plan

Who are you accountable to for your abusive behavior?	What do you need to do to be accountable?	What do you gain from being accountable to this person?	How will you get support to help you remain accountable to this person?

7. To be accountable, you need to commit to specific actions with specific people. Select two people from the list you just made and describe exactly what you will do to become accountable.

1. a. *Who* you will be accountable to:

b. Describe exactly *what* you will do to show that you are accountable:

c. Exactly *when* you will have accomplished this:

2. a. *Who* you will be accountable to:

    b. Describe exactly *what* you will do to show that you are accountable:

    c. Exactly *when* you will have accomplished this:

Goals

In this activity, you will:

1. Better understand the influence of self-talk on your behavior.

2. Increase your positive self-talk.

3. Develop a positive self-talk plan.

Required Worksheet

Self-Talk List (Worksheet 25)

Self-Talk Plan (Worksheet 26)

Self-Talk Record (Worksheet 27)

Notes

1. Check the messages you have said to yourself as you escalated. Add your own to the list:

   ☐ She's out to hurt me.   ☐ I don't give a rip.

   ☐ She doesn't love men.   ☐ She deserves it.

   ☐ She doesn't care about anything.   ☐ It's my house.

   ☐ She's always ragging on me.   ☐ I wish she'd shut up.

   ☐ I'm not angry.   ☐ I can handle my liquor (pot, crack).

   ☐ She's having sex with someone else.   ☐ I'm losing control of her.

   ☐ _____   ☐ _____

   ☐ _____   ☐ _____

2. List the messages you can use to avoid being abusive (see the self-talk list above) in difficult situations.

   a.

   b.

   c.

   d.

You can plan ahead to use positive self-talk. Think of tough situations that often happen to you. List those in the first column. Next, think of all the feelings you might have in each situation (anger, fear, jealousy, and so forth). List these feelings in the middle column. In the final column, write a positive self-talk message to correspond with each feeling.

Situations	Possible feelings	Specific positive self-talk (one for each feeling)

Ways you can remember these self-talk statements:

a.

b.

c.

d.

e.

During the week of _____, record some of the messages you tell yourself:

Date	Message you told yourself	How you felt	What you did	Other messages you could tell yourself

Goals

In this session, you will:

1. Understand what assertiveness means.

2. Understand how assertive behavior is a way of taking responsibility for your actions.

3. Increase your assertiveness skills.

4. Develop an assertiveness plan you can use for many situations.

5. Develop a support system to nurture your assertiveness skills.

Required Worksheets

Ways to Be Assertive (Worksheet 28)

Assertive Actions (Worksheet 29)

How Can You Be Assertive in These Situations? (Worksheet 30)

Assertive Behavior Record (Worksheet 31)

Assertiveness Strategy Plan (Worksheet 32)

Notes

Here are some examples of how some men have chosen to be assertive:

"When you yell at me like that I feel like I'm being treated like a little kid. I am embarrassed and feel stupid. When I feel this way I need to let you know how I feel. I want to be treated like an adult and not yelled at."

"I get worried and angry when you don't return when you say you will and don't call to let me know where you are. I need to tell myself that I can't control what you do or whether you show me that you respect me. I would rather that you at least call and let me know that you are safe."

"I get scared when you say you're going to leave. I need to ask more questions to understand what you mean by 'leaving.' I want you to be honest with me and direct about how you feel."

"When the children act up I get frustrated and confused about how to be a good parent. I need to get time away for a few minutes until I cool down. I want to be open to the needs of my children."

Other examples:

Remember, you are responsible for the effort, not the outcome.

1. List examples of assertiveness in the role-plays:

Scenario One   What did the man do that was assertive?

a.

b.

c.

d.

e.

Scenario Two   What did the man do that was assertive?

a.

b.

c.

d.

e.

Scenario Three   What did the man do that was assertive?

a.

b.

c.

d.

e.

2. What kinds of messages do you give yourself (self-talk) that stop you from being assertive?

3. What kinds of self-talk can you use to be more assertive?

4. Write two examples of situations in which you disagreed with a partner. Then list three ways you could be assertive in each situation:

Situation One

a.

b.

c.

Situation Two

a.

b.

c.

Remember, you are responsible for the effort, not the outcome.

Note: These are additional scenes to use when you practice assertiveness.

1. Your partner answers the phone, whispers into it for a few seconds, then hangs up quickly as you walk into the room.

    a.

    b.

2. Your partner goes to the store and is gone for two hours longer than she said she'd be.

    a.

    b.

3. You and your partner are going to a friend's new home. You wrote down the directions and address, but forgot to bring them with you. Your partner says that she thinks you have gotten them lost.

    a.

    b.

4. You saw a new television that you just had to have. When you bring it home and show your partner, she explains that she just paid the bills two days ago and there was only $27 left in the checking account.

   a.

   b.

5. When you come home from work, you see a strange van parked in your driveway. As you enter the house, you hear voices coming from the bedroom.

   a.

   b.

6. Develop your own scenes:

Remember, you are responsible for the effort, not the outcome.

In what ways were you assertive this week?

Date	Situation	How you felt	What you wanted	How you were assertive	How well you handled the situation	What you gained	What the other person did	Rewards you can give yourself for being assertive

Remember, you are responsible for the effort, not the outcome.

You can improve your assertiveness skills by planning for tough situations. Think of some tough situations that happen again and again. Fill in the chart below as you plan how you can be assertive in each of these situations. This will help you prevent abuse from occurring. Use the tips below the chart to help you plan your assertive responses.

Person involved	Possible situation	How you feel when the situation happens	What you need to do when you feel this way	What you wish would happen in the situation

Following are some tips for being assertive:

1. Use assertive body language
   - Be a comfortable distance from the other person.
   - Take deep breaths before reacting.
   - Take a time-out first, if necessary.
   - Avoid pointing, staring, and standing over someone.
   - Speak in a clear voice.
   - Use "I" statements.

2. Communicate assertively by using the formula below:

    When you (say or do) _____

    _____ ,

    I feel _____

    _____ .

    When I feel this way I need to _____

    _____ .

    I want the situation to be different (or I want you to) _____

    _____ .

3. If the other person does not agree with you, answer the following
    questions for yourself:

    - What can I control about this situation or person?
    - What do I feel now?
    - What do I need to do now?
    - How should I take care of myself in this situation?

Remember, you are responsible for the effort, not the outcome.

Goals

In this activity, you will:

1. Understand the obstacles to relaxing and reducing stress in your life.

2. Develop a plan to reduce stress and maintain some relaxation in your life.

3. Understand how and why to develop a support system for relaxation.

4. Teach yourself to reduce stress and relax.

Required Worksheets

Relaxation Plan (Worksheet 33)
Relaxation Log (Worksheet 34)

Notes

1. What are some obstacles that prevent you from relaxing?

2. Name the five major stresses in your life:

   a.

   b.

   c.

   d.

   e.

3. List the activities you do that are relaxing and help you relieve stress:

4. What are some other things you would like to do for relaxation?

5. Who can you talk to about the above stresses?

Name	Phone #

6. Where can you get some time away for:

1-2 minutes	1-4 hours	1 day to several days

7. List the ways you can work off stress, anxiety, and tension:

8. List some self-talk statements to help you relax:

During the next two weeks, make a commitment to _____ number of
relaxation activities. Record your progress on the chart below:

Date	What you did to relax	For how long	Stress level before relaxing (1-10)*	Stress level after relaxing (1-10)*

*1 = least stressful, 10 = most stressful

Self-Care

Goals

In this activity, you will:

1. Increase your understanding of the options available to build a self-care system.

2. Develop a self-care maintenance plan.

3. Identify parts of your life you want to begin (or continue) to nurture for the sake of your health.

4. Begin a process of daily self-care, rather than living from crisis to crisis.

Required Worksheets

Self-Care Assessment (Worksheet 35)
Self-Care Options (Worksheet 36)
Self-Care Plan (Worksheet 37)

Notes

List some ways you take care of yourself. Then rate how well you take care
of yourself in each of the following categories.

Category	What you do now	How often	Rating (1–5)*
Self-Reward & Self-Talk			
Social			
Relaxation			
Work			
Exercise			
Nutrition			
Assertiveness			
Fun			
Spiritual			
Emotional			

* 1 = not enough; 3 = adequate; 5 = extremely well

Physical Exercise Plan

How can you work off energy or anxiety in a constructive way?
What activities or sports will help?

Relaxation and Stress Reduction Plan

What can you do to relax and think clearly?

Nutrition Plan

What foods and eating patterns will help you relax and think clearly?

Self-Reward & Self-Talk Plan

What positive things can you tell yourself that will help you think clearly?
How can you reward yourself?

Spiritual Plan

What are your spiritual aspects? Where can you go to get more support for
your spirituality? Who are your spiritual role models, and how can you
spend time with them?

Social Plan

What sort of events do you (or could you) attend with friends that are positive and healthy for you? Who are the people in your life that are supportive, encouraging, and positive influences?

Emotional Plan

What ways can you better recognize your feelings? Who can you get support from to be emotional? Who can listen to you express your feelings? How can you see these people regularly? If these people are unavailable, what can you do to support yourself?

Fun Plan

List ways to have fun that are healthy and do not hurt others. Pick three of these that you can do for yourself or with others in the next two weeks.

Assertiveness Plan

What situations regularly come up at work, with your partner, or with your children that require you to be assertive? How can you prepare to be assertive in these situations? (See Worksheets 28-32 for information on how to practice assertiveness.)

List at least two self-care categories you will focus on for the next _____ weeks:

1.

2.

Use the chart below to record your progress in these categories. For each category you choose, record the date and what you did to take care of yourself. For example, if you chose "Physical Exercise," you might write Monday: run 30 minutes; Tuesday: lift weights, and so forth.

Date	Physical Exercise	Relaxation & Stress Reduction	Nutrition	Self-Reward & Self-Talk	Spiritual	Social	Emotional	Fun	Assertiveness

List where or from whom you will get support for maintaining your self-care plan:

1.

2.

3.

4.

Goals

In this activity, you will:

1. Increase your awareness of issues you need to deal with after leaving the program.

2. Increase your awareness of support people and organizations.

3. Develop a support system of people and other resources to deal with a variety of issues.

Building and Maintaining a Support System

Required Worksheet

Building and Maintaining a Support System (Worksheet 38)

Notes

1. List all the people you work with, spend time with, or have contact with in your daily life:

2. Draw a circle around those people with whom you are comfortable making small talk.

3. Next, draw a box around those people with whom you are comfortable talking about your life.

4. Now draw a triangle around those people you can trust with personal information.

5. List all the people from above who you can call for social reasons or in times of crisis. List the names in order of preference, from people you are most likely to call to people you are less likely to call.

6. List the people or organizations you can contact to discuss the following issues:

Family Issues

Divorce	Relationships	Parenting	Childhood experiences

Job Issues

Coworker relationships	Job-related conflicts	Employer relationships

What are some other issues you need to focus on? Look through the list below.
Circle the ones that apply to you and add any that are not included.

- Chemical dependency
- Smoking
- Adult child of an alcoholic
- Family of origin
- Abuse survivor
- Shame
- Building and maintaining relationships

- Nurturing yourself
- Values
- Boundaries
- Self-esteem
- Overly dependent
- Sexism
- Honesty

- Eating
- Emotional health
- Sexuality
- Spirituality
- Intimacy
- Parenting
- Recreation

Where can you get help with these issues?

7. List groups and organizations that you now (or plan to) participate in as part of your support system.

	Name of group	Issue	Time it meets	How often it meets
a.				
b.				
c.				
d.				
e.				

8. List the people you will meet with as part of your individual support system.

	Name	Phone #	How often
a.			
b.			
c.			
d.			
e.			

Goals

In this activity, you will:

1. Better understand and define your personal values.

2. Identify and understand how you model these values for other people.

3. Explore the degree of agreement between your values and your partner's values.

4. Explore what to do when values are not in agreement.

Required Worksheet

Personal Values (Worksheet 39)

Notes

1. Name one person you admire most:

2. List five qualities you admire most about that person:

    a.

    b.

    c.

    d.

    e.

3. List five of your personal values:

    a.

    b.

    c.

    d.

    e.

4. Describe how you show each of these values to other people:

    a.

    b.

    c.

    d.

    e.

5. If you had to choose one value to teach your children, which would it be? Why?

6. How do you model this specific value to your children or others?

7. What are your partner's opinions related to the five values you listed? Does (or did) your partner agree with you?

    a.

    b.

    c.

    d.

    e.

8. What are your children's opinions related to the five values you listed?

   a.

   b.

   c.

   d.

   e.

9. Do other people's values have to be the same as yours? Why or why not?

10. How can you react when someone has an opinion different from yours?

Goals

In this activity, you will:

1. Better understand the effects of parenting.

2. Look at how adults appear to children when violence has occurred in the home.

3. Define discipline and punishment and develop a plan to use disciplining behaviors.

4. Better understand the effects of violence on children.

5. Learn about what can be done for children who have witnessed abuse or who have been abused.

6. Develop a set of parenting values.

Parenting Values

Required Worksheet

Parenting and Discipline (Worksheet 40)

Notes

Once a parent, always a parent.

1. What does it mean to be a parent:

2. How do you demonstrate care for your child(ren):

3. List the differences between punishment and discipline. Which one is
    hurtful? Which is for teaching? Which is more helpful and respectful of
    children? What prevents you from using alternatives to punishment?

Punishment	Discipline

4. In what ways can you provide your child more discipline?

5. Use the behavior change chart below to list some of your children's behaviors that require discipline. In the other columns, write the natural and logical consequences of their behavior and any rewards they might receive by switching to the desired behavior.

Behavior Change Plan

The behavior	Natural consequences	Logical consequences	What you want them to do instead	Rewards

6. Questions to ask yourself as a parent:

   a. What can I control about my child's behavior?

   b. What form of discipline does my child respond to positively?

   Verbally

   Through natural/logical consequences

   Through rewards

   c. How do I feel when my child misbehaves?

d. How do I usually react when my child misbehaves?

e. What support and resources do I need when disciplining my child?

f. What can I do for myself when disciplining my child?

g. What rewards do I receive for using discipline with my child?

h. What negative consequences do I receive for using punishment
    with my child?

Goals

In this activity, you will:

1. Increase your awareness of the dynamics of partner relationships.

2. Better understand and prioritize your needs or expectations in a relationship with a partner.

3. Increase your sense of personal responsibility for your side of the relationship.

Required Worksheet

Relationships (Worksheet 41)

Notes

1. You can learn a lot about relationships by drawing a picture of them. Relationships can be shown by how close or far apart two circles are drawn. Using two circles, draw what your current or most recent relationship with a partner looked like when it began. Label your circle with an "M" and your partner's circle with a "P."

2. Now draw how this relationship looks today:

3. What has changed? What has stayed the same?

4. What does it feel like when your partner wants to move her circle away? How might you react? Who is responsible for your circle (your side of the relationship)?

5. What might you lose if the relationship changes? What might you gain?

6. What are your dreams about how your partner relationships should be?

7. How have you felt when you've realized these dreams would not come true?

8. How can you grieve the losses for changes in your relationship?

    • Who you can talk to:

    • Where you can go:

    • What you can do:

    • What self-talk you can give yourself:

9. List the characteristics you look for and want in a partner (the ideal partner will be...):

10. How many of these expectations can one person meet?

11. List the five characteristics you would rate as most important in a partner. (In other words, what are the five qualities you could not do without.)

    a.

    b.

    c.

    d.

    e.

12. Why are these five important to you?

    a. Because:

    b. Because:

    c. Because:

    d. Because:

    e. Because:

13. If you could add three more, what would they be?

    a.

    b.

    c.

14. What type of person do you feel safest with?

15. What and who is the only thing you can control about the relationship?

16. List the things you've learned about your relationship that will change the way you behave with partners in the future:

17. What has been helpful about looking at your expectations of a partner?

Goals

In this activity, you will:

1. Understand the definition of intimacy, sexuality, and sensuality.

2. Increase your awareness of your needs in each of these three areas.

3. Better understand the barriers to meeting these needs.

4. Develop new possibilities and alternatives for meeting these needs.

Intimacy, Sexuality, and Sensuality

Required Worksheet

Intimacy, Sexuality, and Sensuality (Worksheet 42)

Intimacy Needs Scale (Worksheet 43)

Notes

1. List examples and ideas to define the following terms:

   Intimacy

   Sexuality

   Sensuality

2. Now write examples of how you get these needs met:

   Intimacy

   Sexuality

   Sensuality

3. What are some of the obstacles to getting these needs met?

4. Who first taught you about these terms?

5. When you were growing up, how were boys supposed to show intimacy?

6. When you were growing up, how did you deal with your needs to be sexual?

7. List five ways that being abusive has been an obstacle to getting your
    intimacy, sexuality, and sensuality needs met:

    a.

    b.

    c.

    d.

    e.

8. List five things you can do to meet your intimacy, sexuality, and sensu-
    ality needs without being abusive:

    a.

    b.

    c.

    d.

    e.

Put an "N" on the scale to show where you are *now*.
Put a "W" on the scale to show what you *want*.

Type of Intimacy:	Social	Emotional	Intellectual	Physical & Recreational	Sensual	Affectional	Sexual or Genital	Spiritual
High need 7								
6								
5								
4								
3								
2								
Low need 1								

Adapted from Marilyn J. Mason, Ph.D., Licensed Psychologist, Department of Family Social Science, University of Minnesota Medical School, and author of *Making Our Lives Our Own* (Harper San Francisco) 1986 and coauthor of *Facing Shame: Families in Recovery* (W.W. Norton) 1986.

Self-Esteem and Empowerment

Goals

In this activity, you will:

1. Increase your self-esteem.

2. Better understand which areas of your life you can control.

3. List specific activities that lead to a sense of increased self-worth and empowerment.

Required Worksheet

House of Self-Worth and Empowerment (Worksheet 44)

Notes

1. Label each room in the house below with an aspect of your life that is important to you. (Some examples include *job, family, recreation,* and *friends.*) Then fill each room with specific examples of what you currently do or plan to do to take care of yourself within that category. (For example, under *friends,* you might write, "Continue to keep in touch with my friends.")

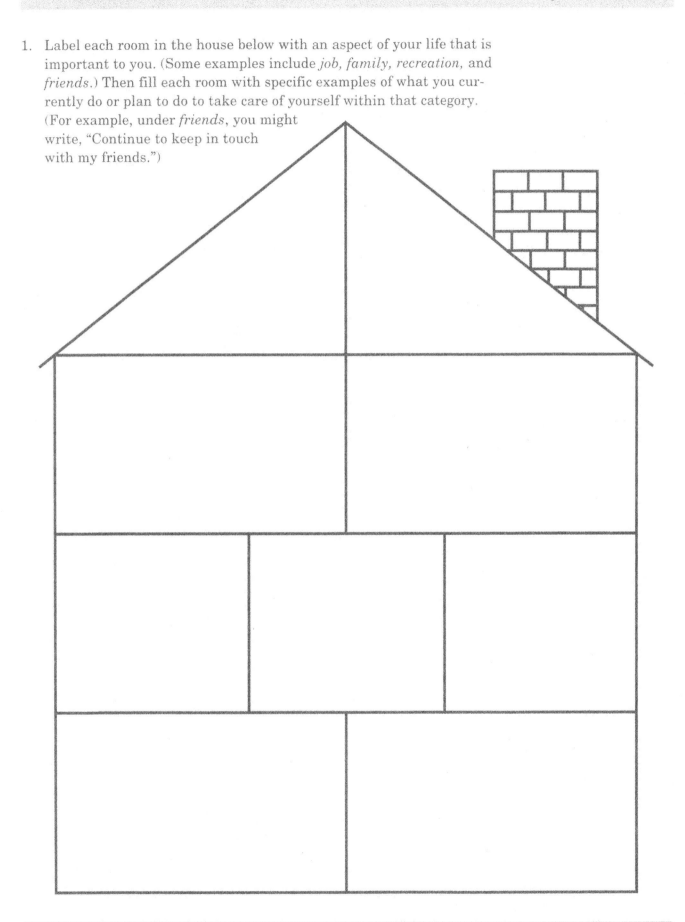

2. What are your feelings when you look at your life this way?

3. What positive actions can you take to fill up these rooms?

Angry Feelings

Goals

In this activity, you will:

1. Become more aware of your feelings of anger, related feelings, and where those feelings originate.

2. Identify varying degrees of anger and the feelings related to anger.

3. Develop a plan to express your anger appropriately.

Required Worksheet

Anger and Abuse (Worksheet 45)

Anger Escalation Log (Worksheet 46)

Notes

1. Anger and abuse are two different things. Draw a picture of each.

Anger	Abuse

2. When you get angry at friends, supervisors, or people at work, how do you let them know you're mad?

3. How do you let your partner know you are angry at her?

4. What are the differences in how you show anger toward other people
   and how you show anger toward your partner?

Other people	Partner

5. What are the similarities in how you show anger toward your partner
   and toward other people?

Other people	Partner

6. What do you do when you are angry at yourself?

7. List specific unhealthy ways you have expressed anger at yourself or others:

8. List specific healthy ways you have expressed your anger:

List two feelings related to anger. Monitor these feelings on this chart for the next week.

Feeling #1: _____

Situation	Intensity (low, medium, high)	Other feelings during this situation	What you were thinking during this situation	What you did when you felt this way	Who you talked with	How you felt after talking about the feelings

Feeling #2:						
Situation						
Intensity (low, medium, high)						
Other feelings during this situation						
What you were thinking during this situation						
What you did when you felt this way						
Who you talked with						
How you felt after talking about the feelings						

Goals

In this activity, you will:

1. Better understand grief and how it affects your behavior.

2. Increase your awareness of your hopes and dreams about a relationship.

3. Understand what dreams you have lost and how you lost them.

4. Understand how loss of dreams may affect your behavior.

5. Gain support for talking about loss and developing new hopes and dreams.

Required Worksheet

Loss of Dreams (Worksheet 47)

Notes

1. List people or things you have lost during your life:

2. Draw the following three pictures:

    a. How you feel when you lose an object.

    b. How you feel when you lose a person.

    c. How you feel when you lose a dream.

3. How do you show these feelings to others?

4. Who can you tell about these feelings?

5. What are some dreams, values, or beliefs about how your relationship with a partner should be?

6. Have you lost some of these dreams about relationships? Which ones?

7. How does it feel to lose these dreams?

8. What dreams do you still have that you may lose?

9. How and where can you get support when you lose a dream?

10. What new dreams do you have about your relationship or future relationships?

Midterm Group Evaluation

Goals

In this activity, you will:

1. Give support, input, concerns, and observations of progress to the other members of the group.

2. Identify, review, reevaluate, or add to your personal goals for this program.

3. Receive constructive suggestions for areas to focus on in the remaining group sessions.

4. Increase your skills in talking directly with your peers about abuse.

Required Worksheet

Midterm Group Evaluation (Worksheet 48)

Notes

1. One thing you have gained from being in this group:

2. One thing that you still want to learn, discuss, focus on, or get support
   for in the remaining sessions:

3. List the strengths and concerns others in the group have stated about you:

Strengths	Concerns

4. Your last word:

Final Group Evaluation

Goals

In this activity, you will:

1. Identify the changes you have made during the group sessions.

2. Better understand the progress you have made and what you have learned through the counseling sessions.

3. Develop a plan for continued nonviolent behavior.

4. Listen to the observations and insights of other group members.

5. Increase your understanding of the need for support and assistance to continue your nonabusive behaviors.

Required Worksheet

Final Group Evaluation (Worksheet 49)

Notes

1. Where were you (emotionally, psychologically) in your life when you started this program?

2. Where are you today?

3. Make a list of *specific* actions you will take to care for yourself and refrain from being abusive:

4. List the suggestions you receive from other group members below:

Strengths	*Concerns*

Printed in the USA
CPSIA information can be obtained
at www.ICGtesting.com
JSHW060045150824
68134JS00031B/2643

9 780940 069060